Th

F. Scott Fitzgerald

Lesson Plan and Study Guides

An Imprint of BookCaps™ Study Guides
www.bookcaps.com

©2012. All Rights Reserved.

Table of Contents

About LessonCaps

LessonCaps is a newly launch imprint of
BookCaps™. Our catalog is quickly growing, so
please stop by our website (**www.bookcaps.com**)
frequently. If there's something we don't have, but
you'd like to read, fill out our contact form and let us
know.

Lesson Plan

Introduction

F. Scott Fitzgerald's *The Great Gatsby* is considered by many to be a quintessential work in American Literature. Originally published in 1925, it captures the spirit of the 1920s, a time of prosperity following World War I. It is narrated in the first-person point of view by Nick Carroway. In addition to traditional literary analysis, teachers of high school students use *The Great Gatsby* to analyze historical context based on the 1920s and to explore issues such as the Prohibition era, societal classes, the women's rights movement, and immigration.

Lesson Plan Format

Each day, students will read a certain number of chapters. Dividing daily readings by chapters instead of pages accounts for different formats students have available to read the book (print and digital.) Using journals, students will respond to a series of questions based on biography and historical context, narrative structure and point of view, characters and character development, and themes, symbols, and figurative language. A listing of homework assignments will give students the opportunity to expand their understanding of *The Great Gatsby*.

Journal

A writing journal is essential to completing the discussion questions and homework assignments for *The Great Gatsby*. Students can purchase journals, or they can create their own personalized journals specifically for the novel. Various websites have instructions for creating foldable writing journals, such as Ehow.com. **(http://www.ehow.com/how_5760860_make-journal-out-paper.html**).

Standards

The Common Core State Standards Initiative (CCSS) is sectioned in five categories for middle and high school students: Reading: Literature, Reading: Informational Text, Writing, Speaking & Listening, and Language (Corestandards.org). The following listed standards correlate to 9th and 10th grade and 11th and 12th classes. Details about the standards are listed on the Common Core State Standards Initiative's website. **(http://www.corestandards.org/the-standards/english-language-arts-standards)**.

Common Core Standards	9-10th Grade	11-12th Grade
Reading: Literature	RL.9-10.1 – RL.9-10.5	RL.11-12.1 – RL.11-12.6, RL.11-12.7, RL.11-12.9
Reading: Informational Text	RI.9-10.1, RI.9-10.5	RI.11-12.1, RI.11-12.5, RI.11-12.6, RI.11-12.7
Writing	W.9-10.1 – W.9-10.10	W.11-12.1 – W.11-12.9
Speaking & Listening	SL.9-10.3, SL.9-10.4, SL.9-10.5	SL.11-12.2, SL.11-12.3, SL.11-12.5
Language	L.9-10.1 – L.9-10.6	L.11-12.1 – L.11-12.6

Sample Rubrics

- **General Rubric Creator (http://rubistar.4teachers.org/)**
- **Acrostic Poem Rubric (http://podcasts.shelbyed.k12.al.us/akessler/files/2012/04/acrostic-poem-rubric.pdf)**
- **Bio Poem Rubric**

(http://www.cpsb.org/Resources/cbt/CBT_0
6-07/station%20activites/MI-
DI/assessment.htm)
- **Collage Rubric**
  (http://www.wdmcs.org/sdrive/Stilwell/Seib
  erling%20-
  %20English/Reading/Book%20Projects/Co
  llage/Collage%20Rubric%20PDF.pdf)
- **Essay Rubric**
  (http://earlycollege.mcsdga.net/documents/
  BasicEssayRubric.pdf)
- **Journal Response Rubric**
  (http://www.readwritethink.org/files/resour
  ces/lesson_images/lesson313/rubric.pdf)
- **PowerPoint Rubric**
  (http://imet.csus.edu/imet6/canet/classes/csu
  s/i_met/284/PPRubric-1.pdf)
- **Venn Diagram Rubric**
  (http://www.readwritethink.org/files/resour
  ces/printouts/VennDiagramRubric.pdf)

Resources Needed

- Copies of *The Great Gatsby*
- Writing journals (purchased or student-created)
- Pens or pencils
- Camera, Smartphone, or Video Recorder (for images and sound)

- Chart paper and copy paper
- Markers or color pencils
- Posterboard

<u>Online</u>

- Biography of F. Scott Fitzgerald
  (**http://www.biography.com/people/f-scott-fitzgerald-9296261**)

This lesson plan refers to following edition of *The Great Gatsby*:

Fitzgerald, F. Scott. *The Great Gatsby*. New York, NY: Scribner, 1995. Print.

Reading Schedule

Day One	Chapters 1-2
Day Two	Chapters 3-4
Day Three	Chapters 5-6
Day Four	Chapters 7
Day Five	Chapters 8-9

Day One: Biography / Historical Context

Objective

Students will be able to better understand how F. Scott Fitzgerald's upbringing and surroundings influences *The Great Gatsby*. They will also explore how gender, economics, and social class impact characters in the novel and current society.

Discussion Questions / Journal Response

1. *The Great Gatsby* was published during the 1920s. Two of the reasons the decade was called the "Roaring Twenties" are because people were able to accumulate wealth and lived "lavish" lifestyles. How does *The Great Gatsby* emulate the idea of the Roaring Twenties? Provide 3-4 examples from the text, with page numbers, in your response.

2. The 1920s heralded some historic changes, including the 1920 ratification of an amendment to the United States Constitution giving women the right to vote (U.S. Constitution Amendment XIX). What role do women play in *The Great Gatsby*? Does Fitzgerald's representation of women reflect a progression of their rights? Why or why not? Include at least three examples, with page numbers, to support your answer.

3. Fitzgerald is credited with coining the term "Jazz Age" in reference to the 1920s. During this time, jazz music became popular, as did clubs playing the genre. How does Fitzgerald use music and clubs in *The Great Gatsby*?

4. In 1920, the ratification of an amendment to the United States Constitution prohibited the sale and manufacturing of alcohol throughout the country (U.S. Constitution Amendment XVIII). Despite Prohibition, people still found ways to obtain alcohol through various means. How is this type of "rebellious" behavior reflected in *The Great Gatsby*? What does the willingness to "break the law" signify?

5. During the 1920s - like the present day - the United States of America dealt with serious issues such as immigration. Hundreds of thousands of immigrants came to the seeking a better life, only to experience discrimination and mistreatment from U.S. citizens. How does *The Great Gatsby* deal with the issue of immigration?

6. Read a biography of F. Scott Fitzgerald in print or online at (**http://www.fscottfitzgeraldsociety.org/biography/index.html**). What aspects of his life are represented in *The Great Gatsby*? Support your points with at least three examples from the text.

7. When *The Great Gatsby* was published in 1925, it was not a commercial success. In fact, it did not become popular until the mid-to-late 1940s. What factors do you think led to the novel's rise in popularity?

8. During his lifetime, F. Scott Fitzgerald faced many disappointments as a writer, playwright, and screenwriter. How does Fitzgerald explore disappointment and failure in *The Great Gatsby*?

Homework Assignments

Links:

- **Bio Poem Format (http://www.readwritethink.org/files/resources/lesson_images/lesson398/biopoem.pdf)**
- **How to write argumentative essays (http://owl.english.purdue.edu/owl/resource/685/05/)**
- **Venn Diagram**

(**http://www.eduplace.com/graphicorganize r/pdf/venn.pdf**)
- **Yahoo Finance (http://finance.yahoo.com/)**

1. Compare and Contrast Essay: During the "Jazz Age" of the 1920s, jazz, which has its roots in the southern part of the United States, became popular throughout the nation. To meet demand, many jazz clubs opened to cater to 1920s party crowds. Research another historical era defined by music. Compare and contrast the Jazz Age and your chosen era. A Venn diagram can help you organize your essay. Use properly documented resources, including the text, to support your points. Your final draft should be 500-750 words. Include a "Works Cited" page with a listing of resources using MLA style.

2. Stock Market Research Paper: The "Roaring Twenties" ended with the Stock Market Crash of 1929, one of the factors that led to the Great Depression of the 1930s. In 2008, the United States faced another significant economic crisis, which included a steep decline in the stock market. Write a 500-750 paper about the 1929 and 2008 stock declines. Explain what factors led to the declines, the economic impact, and the programs the United States government implemented to end the financial crises. Include a "Works Cited" page with a listing of resources using MLA style.

3. Constitutional Amendment Argumentative Essay: During the 1920s, there were constitutional amendments banning the sale of alcohol and granting voting rights to women. Choose an issue affecting people's lives (e.g. texting while driving) and write an argumentative essay asserting why there should be a constitutional ban to address the issue. The completed essay must include your assertion and a minimum of three reasons for your assertion. Use at least three resources to support your assertion. Include a "Works Cited" page with a listing of resources using MLA style.

4. F. Scott Fitzgerald Bio Poem: A bio poem is an 11-line poem that describes a person's life. Each line requires specific information such as the person's name, adjectives that provide descriptive details about the person, and an indispensable relationship. Read a biography of F. Scott Fitzgerald, in print or online. Using the outlined format of a bio poem, create a bio-poem of the author. Use the example as a guide.

5. Comparison Poster: You have been hired to create a poster comparing the 1920s to the 1990s. List at least 10 separate categories to compare the two eras (e.g. clothing). Create a first draft of your chart inside of your writing journal. Draw a three column chart. In the first column, list the categories for your comparisons. In the second column, list examples from the 1920s. The third column will list examples from the 1990s.

Categories	1920s	1990s

Once you complete your first draft, use poster board and your creativity to complete your comparison poster.

6. **Student Investor**: During the 1920s, people invested in stocks as a way to accumulate wealth. Today, investing in the stock market allows people to earn money and prepare for retirement. People invest in stocks for a variety of reasons, including the numbers of years a corporation has existed and the products the corporation manufacturers. If you could buy shares of a corporation, what corporation would you choose? For what reasons? Research the company's stock price. What is its 52-week high? Its 52-week low? Does the company pay dividends (quarterly payouts based on the amount of stocks a person owns)? Based on your research, analyze whether it is a terrific time to purchase shares.

Day Two: Narrative / Structure / Point of View

Objective

Students will be able to better understand the narrative structure of *The Great Gatsby*. They will also explore the effectiveness of F. Scott Fitzgerald's use of the first-person point of view.

Discussion Questions / Journal Response

1. In Chapter 3, Nick states, "Why has it all got to come through Miss Baker" (76). Nick is exasperated because Gatsby will not tell him what he wants. Why does Fitzgerald use Nick to facilitate the reunion between Daisy and Gatsby? What elements does this add to the novel?

2. The narrator is an instrumental voice in a story. He can gain the reader's trust or skepticism from the beginning of a written work. Does Nick Calloway gain the reader's trust or skepticism as the narrator? Provide specific examples in your response. How do you think the story would differ if it were narrated from a different point of view?

3. In *The Great Gatsby*, Fitzgerald uses first-person narration through Nick to explore his point of view. How does telling the story from Nick's point of view allow Fitzgerald to make critical judgments about class in the Unites States during this time period? How might the perspective be different if it were told from someone equal in class to the Buchanans?

4. Fitzgerald makes a point of mentioning the Daisy's daughter but never features her. What interactions are noted between Daisy and her daughter? What do these interactions show? What kind of mother does Daisy appear to be? Explain your answer using evidence from the text.

5. Social entertaining is a gigantic part of this novel. What are some instances of social entertaining in the novel? Why is entertaining such a large part of the lives of some of the characters? Gatsby is known for his parties. Why does he have so many parties? Are the party scenes related to the organization of the novel? Why or why not?

6. Fitzgerald's fictional East and West Egg present a subtle contrast of classes. How does Gatsby's real background differentiate from the upper echelon of West Egg society? Is this difference obvious despite Jay's wealth? Why is Gatsby not perceived as upper crust in West Egg? How does exploring this contrast contribute to the effectiveness of the novel?

7. The depiction of the relationship between Tom Buchanan and Myrtle Wilson sets up a sympathetic tone towards Daisy early in the novel. How does the author's description of this relationship affect the reader's feelings about Daisy's subsequent relationship with Gatsby? Is this an intentional organizational strategy by the author? Why or why not?

8. All novels have a conflict, a problem that must be resolved. The conflict is generally introduced during the rising action of a novel. What is the main conflict of the story? How does Fitzgerald present this conflict?

Homework Assignments

Links:

- **Interactive Plot Diagram (http://www.readwritethink.org/files/resources/interactives/plot-diagram/)**
- **Online Flash Card Maker (http://www.kitzkikz.com/flashcards/)**
- **Printable Plot Diagram (http://www.thinkport.org/31701409-ec7e-40a9-9ae2-176a3c7d0508.asset?)**
- **Storyboard Templates**

(**http://www.the-flying-animator.com/storyboard-template.html**)
- **T-chart graphic organizer**
  (**http://www.eduplace.com/graphicorganizer/pdf/tchart_eng.pdf**)

1. Plot Pyramid Chart: All stories have plots - sequence of events. Sometimes plots can be linear, action happens in a sequenced order, or non-linear, action is not recorded in the order that it happened. Create a plot pyramid based on *The Great Gatsby* using a printable or interactive plot diagram from ReadWriteThink.org. Continue to work on the plot pyramid throughout the story. Make sure to include the exposition, rising action, climax, falling action and resolution.

2. Point of View Rewrite: The point of view of a text has a significant impact on the reader's perception of the action in a story. Reread Chapter 3. Rewrite a portion of the chapter in first-person point of view using Gatsby as the narrator. Then, write a paragraph explaining how changing the narrator impacts the novel.

3. **Imagery Drawing Activity**: Imagery in text creates a sensory experience for the reader. Fitzgerald uses imagery, language that appeals to the five senses, to help the reader visualize the action in the story. Review the beginning of chapter 3 of *The Great Gatsby*. Create a visual representation of the scene as Nick walks over to Gatsby's party. Use chart paper and colored pencils to create the vivid colors and scenery that Fitzgerald writes about. Then write a paragraph in your journal explaining how the imagery in the text helps you to visualize the scene.

4. Character's Point of View Activity: On a sheet of copy paper create a chart with two columns. In the first column, list a minimum of three characters from the text. In the second column write one word that describes Nick's feelings about the character. At the bottom of the page, write one paragraph eight to ten sentences long justifying why your descriptive words are accurate.

5. Letter: After Nick moves to Long Island, he finds himself among elite company in West Egg. Write a letter (200-350 words) from Nick to his parents. Use the letter as a means to explain what Nick experiences in West Egg.

6. Flash Cards: Using note cards create a set of flashcards to help understand point of view terms. First, write the term on the front of the card and the definition on the back.

The Great Gatsby is written in first person point of view. Choose a phrase from the novel that clearly shows the point of view. Modify the phrase on each card to reflect that particular point of view. The original phrase should appear on the first person point of view card.

Terms are **first person**, **second person**, **third person limited**, and **third person omniscient**.

7. Journal writing: Reflecting on a text helps the reader to make text to text and text to life connections. This is one of the habits of mind that proficient readers have. Reread the Chapter 4 and reflect over the narrator's description of Gatsby's Sunday party and the people who attend. Write a response (200-300 words) to the chapter.

Day Three: Characters and Character Development

Objective

Students will be able to identify the protagonist and the antagonist in *The Great Gatsby*. They will be able to identify character traits of major and minor characters. They will be able to analyze how the characters' actions and descriptions contribute to the overall structure of *The Great Gatsby*.

Discussion Questions / Journal Response

1. While Jay Gatsby and the Buchanans are wealthy, they are obviously from different worlds. Explain the differences in their classes. Why do these differences exist despite their wealth? Is there a bridge between old money and new money and how does one cross it?

2. While Nick is the narrator, he seems to be totally different from most of the other characters in the novel. What accounts for the differences in Nick? What character traits could be used to describe Nick? Use evidence from the text to support your answer. What is Nick's role in the action of the novel? Is his character necessary? Why or why not?

3. In chapter two, Nick meets Tom Buchanan's mistress, Myrtle. Tom breaks Myrtle's nose for speaking of his wife, Daisy. Based on this incident, what are three character traits that describe Tom Buchanan? Use evidence from the text to support your answer.

4. Jay Gatsby is the namesake of the novel. Why is the novel named for this particular character? What are some of the notable characteristics of Jay Gatsby? Why does the author not give a lot of information about Gatsby at the beginning of the novel? What quality does it add to the character? Why?

5. Why does Nick pursue a friendship with Jordan Baker? Does he have any real interest in her as a woman? Is there anything that interferes with his pursuit of Jordan? If so, what is it? What are Jordan's reasons for pursuing Nick?

6. Tom Buchanan and Jay Gatsby are two principal characters in the novel. How are the characters similar? How are they different? Under normal circumstances, is it likely that these characters would become friends? Why or why not?

7. Daisy Buchanan is a typical wife in East Egg. What challenges does she face in her marriage to Tom? Does Daisy appear to be a happy with her life as a wife and mother? Use evidence from the text to support your answer.

8. Jordan seems to believe that Daisy is missing something in her life and plans to do something about it. What might Daisy be missing? How does Jordan plan to add this extra element to Daisy's life? Should Jordan interfere in this manner?

9. The reader learns a lot of fascinating information regarding Jay Gatsby. What techniques does Fitzgerald use to develop this character? How is Gatsby an instrumental character in this novel? What details does Fitzgerald use to engage the reader regarding Gatsby's character?

10. A static character is a character that does not change over the course of a story. Identify at least one static character. Why do you believe this character does not change? How could this character become a dynamic character? Give evidence from the text to support your answer.

Homework Assignments

Links:

- **Interactive Acrostic Poem Maker (http://www.readwritethink.org/files/resources/interactives/acrostic/)**
- **Interactive Literary Elements Map (Interactive Literary Elements Map)**

- **Interactive Venn Diagram (http://www.readwritethink.org/files/resources/interactives/venn/)**
- **Online Collage Maker (http://www.photovisi.com/)**
- **Online Social Network Profiler (http://www.readwritethink.org/classroom-resources/student-interactives/profile-publisher-30067.html)**

1. Essay: Jay Gatsby is an attractive and popular personality. Everyone wants to come to his parties, and no one wants to leave when they are over. Write an essay, (350-500 words) explaining why people are so attracted to Jay Gatsby's character. Use specific examples from the text to support your points.

2. Acrostic Poem: An acrostic poem is organized by a series of lines where the beginning letter of each line spells another word. All lines of the poem should relate to or describe the main topic. Choose one character from the reading to create an acrostic poem in your journal. The original topic may be either the name of the character, something that specifically relates to the character, or a character trait of the character.

3. Compare and Contrast: In *The Great Gatsby*, Fitzgerald weaves a complex web of characters. Explore the similarities and differences between Jay Gatsby and Tom Buchanan by using an **http://www.readwritethink.org/files/resources/interactives/venn/**interactive or print version of a Venn diagram to compare and contrast their character traits. Your completed Venn diagram should include at least 6 differences and 4 similarities.

4. Character Image Collage: A collage is an art form in which compositions are made out of pieces of cloth, paper, and photographs. Create a collage on a piece of chart paper. Find pictures that clearly represent either one character or a variety of characters from the text. Collages should consist of no less than twenty-five pictures. A one page explanation of the collage should be completed in student journals.

5. Chalk it Up: Exploring the characteristics, actions and motivations of a character adds to the reader's overall understanding of a text. Choose one character from the text to explore. Draw a chalk outline of a person in your journal or on a blank sheet of copy paper. Chart out the characteristics on the outline in the following manner: (1) List the emotional characteristics near the heart; (2) List the mental or behavioral characteristics in the head; (3) Use the limbs to list the character's physical characteristics. Beside the characteristics, give evidence from the text to support your description, as well as a page number. Once you complete the chart outline, use it to write a one page character analysis (350-500 words).

6. Character Map: Exploring a character deeply requires looking at physical characteristics, thoughts and motivations. Choose one of the characters from *The Great Gatsby* and create a character map using an interactive literary elements map from ReadWriteThink.org. Write a paragraph in your journal describing the character in detail.

7. Social Network Profile: Social networks offer an opportunity to connect with family and old friends and to meet new people. Use an interactive profile publisher to create a social networking profile. Choose a character from *The Great Gatsby*. Make sure that the text gives enough information about the chosen character to create an attractive profile. Enter information about the character into the profile publisher. Make sure that information is accurate. In your journal, write a paragraph (100-200 words) explaining what inferences you can make about the character based on the social networking profile.

Day Four: Themes / Symbols / Figurative Language

Objective

Students will explore the themes of wealth and social class in *The Great Gatsby*. They will identify symbols in the novel and explore how Fitzgerald uses alliteration, simile, metaphor, and personification.

Discussion Questions / Journal Response

1. Nick's first meeting with Gatsby occurs at a party. What is ironic about Nick's first meeting with Gatsby? Does Gatsby appear to have an ulterior motive for being polite to Nick? Use evidence from the text to explain your answer.

2. At the end of Chapter 1, there is a cryptic mention of "a single green light" (26). What does this single green light symbolize? Use evidence from the text to explain your answer. What are some other symbols used in *The Great Gatsby*? What is the significance of those symbols?

3. At the beginning of Chapter 2, Fitzgerald references a valley of ashes where "men move dimly and already crumbling through the powdery air" (27). What does the "valley of ashes" symbolize? This valley lies between East and West Egg. Is there any significance in the description of the valley? Why or why not?

4. Fitzgerald uses a variety of figures of speech in *The Great Gatsby*. Review at minimum of two chapters and find examples of figurative language. List the examples in your journal and identify the types of figurative language used. Explain the effects of figurative language on the reader's understanding of the text.

5. The introduction of Tom and Myrtle Wilson in the novel gives a glimpse of the importance of social class in the novel. What class can be used to describe Tom and Myrtle? Why? Is the couple content with their position in society? What message does Fitzgerald send about societal classes in *The Great Gatsby*?

6. The relationship between Tom Buchanan and Myrtle Wilson seems to win the approval of several people even though they are both married. Is this relationship in any way a threat to their marriages? Why or why not? What message is Fitzgerald trying to send by his development of the relationship between these two characters?

7. Living the "American dream" is a saying used frequently in this society. Are any of the characters the epitome of the American dream? If so, who and why? If not, how can a character reach the American dream? Is there a message in this text about the difficulties inherent in attaining the "dream?" If so, what is it?

8. Fitzgerald's fictional cities of East and West Egg present a subtle contrast of classes. West Egg is an unfashionable area inhabited by people with new money. On the other hand, East Egg's residents are the product of century old money. What are some of the subtle differences in these two groups of people? Why might West Egg's residents feel superior to East Egg's residents? Is there still a gap between old and new money in this country? Why or why not?

9. Even though Jay Gatsby has made a vast deal of money, it does not afford him entry into the highest levels of society. Does Jay Gatsby appear to care about class? Why or why not? Is his money only a means to an end? Use evidence from the text to explain your answer. Could he ever reach the upper society that he hangs on the fringe of? Why or why not?

10. While there are usually several themes in a novel, there is generally an overwhelming message in the book. What is the overall theme of the book? What devices does Fitzgerald use to punctuate this theme?

Homework Assignments

<u>Link</u>:

- **Classification Organizer Printable (http://education.nationalgeographic.com/education/multimedia/classification-chart/?ar_a=1)**
- **Online Collage Maker (http://www.photovisi.com/)**

1. **Figurative Language Classification**: A simile is a comparison of unlike things using like or as. A metaphor is a comparison of, unlike things. Personification occurs when inanimate objects are given human characteristics. Alliteration is repetition of consonant sounds at the beginning of words. Complete a **http://education.nationalgeographic.com/education/multimedia/classification-chart/?ar_a=1**classification organizer using examples of figurative language from *The Great Gatsby*. Find at least five examples of each type of figurative language. Label each square with one type of figurative language and place the examples in the appropriate squares along with the appropriate page number.

2. **Write a Narrative**: A compelling narrative tells a story. It engages the reader from beginning to ending with a deliberate hook, colorful characters, figurative language, a well thought out plot and a clear theme. Write a narrative about a person who has a secretive past. Please make sure that your narrative includes all of the following:

- An engaging beginning
- A protagonist with a mysterious personality
- Five to six examples of imagery
- At least five examples of figurative language (similes, metaphors, personification, onomatopoeia, hyperbole, and etc)
- An imaginative plot
- A clear theme

The narrative should be organized into paragraphs and written into the journal.

3. **Short Essay**: All narratives have a theme, a universal message about life. After completing the novel, write a theme statement that reflects the message about life in the novel. In a short essay (350-400 words), explain the theme(s) explored in *The Great Gatsby*. Use examples from the text to support your ideas. Make sure that your essay is well developed and complete.

4. **Figurative Language Collage**: Figurative language engages the reader in a literary work. It makes a text come alive for the reader. Create a mini-figurative language collage. Find two or three examples of each type of figurative language: similes, metaphors, and personifications. Write the quotes on sheet of copy paper. You can use text boxes for your quotes. Label each example. Cut the quotes out and glue them to a sheet of construction paper.

5. **Long Essay**: Write an essay (1000-1500 words) discussing how Fitzgerald uses imagery in the text. Your introductory paragraph should include a thesis. Your concluding paragraph will summarize your essay's main points. Make sure to cite examples of imagery from the text to support your essay. Include a "Works Cited" page with a listing of resources using MLA style.

6. **Found Poem**: In "found poems," writers take a text, pull out pieces that resonate with them, and reorganize the pieces into a poetic structure. Write a found poem based on Chapter 7. Find two examples of figurative language on each page of the chapter. Arrange the example in any order that you choose. Write your final poem on a separate sheet of copy paper. Then, write a reflection describing how writing the poem impacted your understanding of the writer's use of figurative language.

Day Five: Book Review

Objective

Students will analyze several aspects of *The Great Gatsby* as they explore how the novel impacts society based on reader reception. Students will examine critical reviews of the novel as well as dramatic adaptations in order to gain an understanding of different perspectives of *The Great Gatsby*.

Discussion Questions / Journal Response

1. *The Great Gatsby* was published in 1925. Although ninety-seven years have passed since its release, it is still required reading for many students. What makes the book so popular? Does it still resonate with today's readers? Why or why not?

2. Given the social, economic, and political circumstances on the 1920s, what message was Fitzgerald attempting to send with this novel? Where was his message directed? Does the novel convey the same message to today's readers?

3. What are positive aspects of the book? What are negative aspects of the book? Use three examples in your response.

4. Myrtle Wilson and Jay Gatsby die at the end of the novel. The deaths, as well as the callousness of Gatsby's associates, affect Nick negatively. What advice would you offer to Nick? Why?

5. Imagine you could prevent one of the characters from a destructive end. Which character would you choose to save to why?

6. What are the most engaging parts of *The Great Gatsby*? Give three detailed reasons. Which parts of the novel is the least interesting? Explain why? What would you do to improve it?

.

7. Development of characters is instrumental to pen an engaging novel. How does Fitzgerald's development of the characters make *The Great Gatsby* a compelling novel? Are there any characters that needed more development? Why or why not?

8. When *The Great Gatsby* was released in 1925, it did not sell enough copies to be considered a successful novel. Like many of Fitzgerald's works, it gained popularity after his death. If *The Great Gatsby* were published today, do you think it would be a bestselling novel? Why or why not?

Homework Assignments

<u>Links</u>:

- Online Book Cover Creator (**http://www.readwritethink.org/files/resources/interactives/bookcover/**)
- Online Cube Creator (**http://www.readwritethink.org/files/resources/interactives/cube_creator/**)
- Printable Cube Pattern (**http://printables.atozteacherstuff.com/435/cube-pattern/**)
- Word Web Graphic Organizer (**http://www.eduplace.com/graphicorganizer/pdf/clusterweb2.pdf**)

(1) Eulogy: A eulogy is a speech given at a funeral about the deceased person. At the end of *The Great Gatsby*, Jay Gatsby is killed. Pretend that you are Nick and write a eulogy for Jay Gatsby. Make sure that you include the following in the eulogy:

- Examples of Jay Gatsby's dialogue
- Nick's feelings about Gatsby
- Biographical information about Gatsby's life
- Some details about how others have responded to Gatsby's death

2. **Personal Dictionary**: Understanding the definition of words used in a text is a necessary part of comprehension. To truly understand new words, it is imperative to associate words with other familiar words (synonyms). In your journal, create a personal dictionary using unfamiliar terms in the novel. Choose two terms from each vignette. Look up each term. Use a word web graphic organizer as a template, complete the following tasks: (1) enter the unknown word in the center, (2) the definition in context in the top left bubble, (3) the part of speech in the middle left bubble, (4) a sentence in the top right bubble, (5) a sentence using the middle right bubble, and (6) a visual representation in the bottom right bubble.

3. **The Great Gatsby Commercial**: Starmark Studios is releasing an adaptation of *The Great Gatsby* in movie theaters early 2013. The company hires you to write a script and direct a 1 minute commercial to convince moviegoers to come see the movie when it is released. Produce a 1-minute commercial promoting the "upcoming" *The Great Gatsby* movie.

4. **The Book v.** _____: Like many bestselling novels, *The Great Gatsby* has been adapted for dramatic productions such as plays and movies. When a novel is adapted, playwrights and screenwriters will modify scenes from a novel, add or set aside characters, and even change endings. Find a dramatic adaptation of The Great Gatsby. After viewing the adaptation, write an essay (350-500 words) exploring the differences between the novel and the adaptation.

5. **Diorama**: A diorama is a miniature three dimensional scene. Choose one scene from *The Great Gatsby* that can be reproduced in a diorama. Using a shoebox or similar container, recreate the scene as accurately as possible.

6. **Book Jacket**: Book jackets create anticipation in the reader. They are visually captivating and build tension. Using an interactive book cover from ReadWriteThink.org, choose full dust jackets. Enter the information as requested by the creator. You can also choose to use copy paper to create your own book jacket. Make sure that your book jacket is a hook to draw the reader.

7. **Story Cube**: A creative way to summarize a novel is a story cube. Using the online or printable cube creator, create a story cube that depicts the action in *The Great Gatsby*. If using the online version, enter information in the cube until all six categories have a check. Once you finish the cube, print your completed copy and fold it into the desired shape. If you use the printable, fill in each side, cut out the figure and fold as necessary. Be creative!

8. **Personal Book Review**: After completing *The Great Gatsby*, write a book review (500-700 words). The essay should address the following: summarize of the book, address the elements of plot, outline good and bad points about the book, and explain whether or not you would recommend the book and why.

9. **Opinion Pieces**: Research book critics' reviews of *The Great Gatsby*. Write a short essay summarizing the critics' main points, based on favorable and unfavorable opinions. Include a paragraph explaining whether you agree with the favorable or unfavorable opinions. Use specific examples to support your points. Include a "Works Cited" page with a listing of resources in MLA style.

Lesson Plan References

Fitzgerald, F. Scott. *A Short Autobiography*. Ed.
James L.W. West III. New York, NY: Scribner, 2011.
Print.

Fitzgerald, F. Scott. *The Great Gatsby*. New York,
NY: Scribner, 1995. Print.

Johnson, Claudia. *Class Conflict in F. Scott
Fitzgerald's The Great Gatsby*. Farmington Hills,
        MI: Greenhaven, 2008. Print

Weisbold, Eva. *A Student's Guide to F. Scott
Fitzgerald.* Berkeley Heights, NJ:
        Scribner, 2004. Print.

Please note: Other resources are listed and available
under "links" in the "homework assignment" sections
of this lesson plan.

Study Guide

Historical Context

F. Scott Fitzgerald was born Francis Scott Key Fitzgerald in St. Paul, Minnesota in 1896. He was named after his ancestor, Francis Scott Key, who wrote the "Star Spangled Banner". He was very smart as a child, but he did not do well in school, so he was sent to boarding school in New Jersey in 1911. Despite the fact that he was only an average student, he was accepted to Princeton University. He had a terrible time in college and dropped out in 1917 to join the army, just as World War I was ending. He was stationed in Alabama where he fell in love with a seventeen-year-old girl named Zelda who would not marry him until he became successful. Armed with the determination to make something of himself and marry Zelda, Fitzgerald published his first novel, "This Side of Paradise" (1920), which made him an instant literary success and Zelda agreed to marry him.

In 1925 Fitzgerald published his most famous novel, "The Great Gatsby" which was loosely based on some events of his earlier life, such as his education at an Ivy League school and meeting the love of his life while stationed in the South. In the "roaring twenties" Fitzgerald spent his money on fruitless possessions and throwing wild parties, which is something that Jay Gatsby does to try to win the love of Daisy in the novel. Fitzgerald became one of the most well-known writers for chronicling life in the 1920's. He was driven by a love for life and adventure during this time, but it ended too soon as his alcoholism and unhealthy lifestyle cause him to die of a heart attack at the age of forty-four.

Plot

Nick Carraway, the narrator, is from the Midwest but moves himself to Long Island for work. He lives in an area known as West Egg, where the people of "new money" live. It is across the bay from East Egg where the more fashionably rich people reside. Nick's cousin Daisy Buchanan and her husband Tom live in East Egg where they spend their days with their friend Jordan, entertaining the high society. Nick lives next door to a mysterious man named Jay Gatsby who throws the most lavish parties at which he rarely makes an appearance. When Nick finally meets Gatsby the two form a fast friendship and Nick finds out that Gatsby is in love with Daisy, whom he has known for a long time. Daisy's husband Tom has been cheating on her for their entire marriage, currently with a woman named Myrtle Wilson whose husband owns the auto garage where Tom and Nick stop on a trip to the city. Nick feels very uncomfortable in this dishonest crowd of people, though he is slightly intrigued by the dangerous web they have all woven around and between themselves. As the secrets and affairs begin to unravel Nick finds himself as a front-row observer in tragedy resulting from jealousy. When Tom's mistress, Myrtle, is struck by Gatsby's car and killed he allows Wilson to believe that Myrtle was having an affair with Gatsby, rather than himself; little does Tom know that his wife was driving the car that killed Myrtle. Wilson, seeking revenge for the affair as well as his wife's death, kills Gatsby and then himself. Nick realizes that he is disgusted by the world he has immersed himself in and decides to move back West.

Themes

Social Class

Social Class is important to everyone in this novel, even Nick who tries to stay unaffected by his surroundings. The neighborhoods of West Egg and East Egg are separated by a bay, and also by the financial status of the people living in either. The people of West Egg are "new money" while the people of East Egg are snobbier and of old wealth. When Tom finds out that Daisy is having an affair he is not so much upset by the affair as he is with the fact that she is having an affair with someone who is not of the appropriate class. There is some talk of "marrying down" as well, mostly relating to Myrtle and her mechanic husband George.

Love

Love is a complicated concept within this novel because it seems that no one really loves anyone else as much as they love themselves. Gatsby believes that he loves Daisy, but he does not realize, as Nick does, that he only loves the memory he has of Daisy, not who she has become. Daisy feels as though she loves Gatsby, but it becomes increasingly clear that she does not love anyone, she only loves the idea of someone loving her. It is obvious that Tom does not love anyone, but is a total womanizer who simply wants all of the women in his life to be with him exclusively. Even Nick, who is easily the most level-headed of the bunch, only "half-loves" Jordan.

Deceit

The magnitude of lies and deceit in this novel is astounding. There are so many ill-kept secrets and deceptions that it is almost difficult to keep track of them all. All of the couples seem to have toxic relationship filled with disillusions. Tom has had numerous affairs throughout his marriage to Daisy, Daisy does not even try to hide her affair with Gatsby, Tom lets George think that Myrtle is having an affair with Gatsby rather than him, and Nick seems to be skeptical of everything that people tell him, because he knows that their lives revolve around lies and gossip.

Wealth

Wealth is all that really matters to the shallow characters of this novel. Everyone moves to the Eggs or hangs out with people who live in the Eggs either because they are wealthy or because they desperately want to be. Wealth is a symbol of success to Tom and most of the people he associates with and to Gatsby it is a means of being accepted by Daisy. Gatsby decorates his entire grand house in the most expensive things he can find just to impress Daisy, not realizing that if she only cares about his financial status then she does not actually love him at all.

Memory

Memory works in mysterious ways for the characters here. Nick seems to have an impossible time remembering anything from his past. There are several instances where he is reminded of something he heard or experienced before, but he has a hard time recalling exactly what that was. For Gatsby, it seems he is ruled by his memory and the past is all he cares about. He remembers the Daisy he fell in love with years ago, and he assumes that she is the same person he knew then, not willing to accept that she does not love him, she just loves being adored.

Morality

Nick is the only voice of morality in this novel and the only character that seems to have a conscience at all. Gatsby sees no problem with the fact that he told several white lies to get him closer to Daisy, or that he became a bootlegger to make himself financially successful and thereby desirable in Daisy's eyes. The couples within the novel seem to have no problem cheating on one another, or in the case of Daisy and Tom, causing reckless behaviors and then running away from the aftermath rather than clean the mess up themselves.

Gender Roles

There is a definite double standard when it comes to the actions of men versus the actions of women within the novel though the 1920's do mark a more liberal time for women. Tom seems to have no problem with his sexual liberalism, and with the fact that he has an affair with a woman below his social class, but when it comes to Daisy's affair Tom is furious, especially as he finds Gatsby to be below him on the social scale. Possibly because of the changing roles of woman in the 1920's or because the characters are wealthy, Daisy and Jordan do not fit gender stereotypes as they spend their days gossiping, drinking, and in Jordan's case golfing.

Education

Education is very important in terms of fitting in with the social scene. There is a great importance placed on where a man received his education. Nick is automatically accepted into the social scene, despite the fact that he lives in West Egg because he is Daisy's cousin and also because he has an Ivy League education. Gatsby tells people that he attended Oxford, which it is revealed to be not exactly a lie, but is an exaggeration because he only attended for a couple months. Tom is appalled by Gatsby's lack of elite education to the point that he sees him as a lesser man.

Dissatisfaction

All of the characters in the novel are dissatisfied with their lives in a certain way. Tom and Daisy are obviously not getting what they need from their relationship, which causes them to seek extramarital relationships. Tom seeks the affection of many women while Daisy seeks the adoration of any man will give her the attention she needs. Jordan feels the need to brag about her life, but at the same time cannot help but gossip about the lives of others whom she appears to live vicariously through. Even Nick, who seems grounded in comparison to the others, is dissatisfied to the point that he is trying to find a place where he feels content.

The American Dream

The American Dream is shot down here, as the privileged individuals are exposed as being the most dissatisfied with their lives. Gatsby's goal throughout his life, as is revealed by his father, is to make something grand of his life and to be financially successful. He achieves this goal by lying his way to the top, though he does it, not for himself but to make Daisy love him. Daisy and Tom are already wealthy, living the American Dream, but they have a broken and abusive marriage which results in quite a bit of drinking and extramarital affairs. The American Dream is clearly not all it is cracked up to be as it results in lies, deceit, and tragedy.

Characters

Nick Carraway

Nick is the narrator who is twenty-nine at the start of the novel. He is from the Midwest but has recently moved to the West Egg area of Long Island to pursue his career in bonds. He is accepted into high society because of his Ivy League education and his relation to Daisy Buchanan who is a high society Queen Bee. As he befriends the mysterious Jay Gatsby he realizes the disgusting, and shallow realities of living the American Dream and the lengths that people will go to achieve happiness and success when they are able to get away with anything.

Jay Gatsby

Jay Gatsby (birth name James Gatz) is a mysterious man who lives in the West Egg right next door to Nick. He throws the most lavish parties though he is rarely seen. Jay has been in love with Daisy for many years and has achieved a life of success through white lies and illegal activities in order to make her fall in love with him again, despite her marriage to Tom Buchanan. Jay, as Nick points out, has spent all of his time reaching for a goal that lies in the past rather than in the future. Despite the fact that Daisy is obviously only interested in being adored, regardless of who is doing the adoring.

Daisy Buchanan

Daisy is the cousin of Nick and the object of Gatsby's undying love. The impression given is that Daisy is a unique sort of girl with a voice that is special and always rings of excitement. She loved Gatsby when she was a young woman but ended up marrying Tom Buchanan, who has always been unfaithful and abusive toward her. In an effort to find the adoration, she has been craving Daisy has an affair with Gatsby. Daisy ends up staying with Tom in the end because Tom can provide her the life that she has always known, rather than the life of spontaneity and unexpectedness that Gatsby would provide.

Tom Buchanan

Tom is Daisy's abusive and unfaithful husband. Right after they were married, he had an affair with a hotel maid and at the time of the novel he was having an ongoing relationship with a woman named Myrtle Wilson. Tom is shallow and a snob, who thinks that people who are not of inherited money or who have not had an Ivy League education are not worthy of his time or of his social circle. Tom is extremely selfish, finding no fault in his own extramarital affairs but furious over Daisy's affair with Gatsby. He convinces his mistress' husband that Gatsby was the one she was having an affair with, which leads to the death of both Gatsby and George Wilson.

Jordan Baker

Jordan is a professional women's golfer and Daisy's best friend. Jordan is as deceptive as anyone, which makes her more acutely aware of the deceptions of others that any of the other characters. She is extremely cynical and believes nothing that anyone says, especially Jay Gatsby. She is beautiful, self-centered and independent, and she starts a relationship with Nick, whom she finds to be one of the few honest people, though she changes her mind at the end of the novel. Jordan, always critical of the actions of others, is known to have lied in order to win her first golf tournament.

Myrtle Wilson

Myrtle Wilson is married to George Wilson and has been involved in a longtime affair with Tom Buchanan. Myrtle feels sorry for herself for marrying a man who owns a run-down garage and is going nowhere in life and tries to improve her situation by having an affair with someone who is of a higher class. Unfortunately for her, Myrtle chooses Tom to have an affair with, and Tom is far too stuck up to leave his high society wife for a woman like Myrtle, though he makes her promises to keep her around. She accepts Tom's abuse as a sign of masculinity, something George is lacking in her opinion.

George Wilson

George is the husband of Myrtle. He owns a run-down auto repair shop that sits on the edge of the Valley of Ashes. He loves his wife very much, and when he finds out that she is having an affair he is devastated; his devastation is only made worse when Myrtle is killed by whoever is driving Gatsby's yellow Rolls Royce. George allows Tom to convince him that Gatsby is the man who Myrtle is cheating with and George tracks Gatsby down and kills him, then turns the gun on himself. George is sympathetic character who is actually quite a bit like Gatsby in that they both are dreamers who are unfalteringly in love with women who are in love with Tom.

Meyer Wolfsheim

Wolfsheim is Gatsby's shady business partner. He is known to be a key player in the organized crime world and is rumored to have rigged the World Series of 1919. It is the Wolfsheim's character, which makes the reader, and the other characters, wonder how Gatsby really made all of his money. Wolfsheim is the person who got Gatsby into the bootlegging of illegal alcohol and their continued relationship with one another leads Nick, and the reader, to believe that Gatsby must still have a hand in the business. Wolfsheim does not bother to show for Gatsby's funeral, which Nick finds both unfortunate and disrespectful.

Owl Eyes

Owl Eyes is a character that Nick meets at his first party at Gatsby's home. He encounters the man in the library where he admits that he has not been sober for a week and hopes that being surrounded by books will sober him up. He appears to be in awe that so many books exist in place and that they are all real. The night of that party he crashes his car into a wall while he is leaving the drive way and loses a wheel. To Nick's immense surprise the only one of Gatsby's acquaintances who attends his funeral other than himself is Owl Eyes.

Klipspringer

Klipspringer is a freeloader who lives in Gatsby's home most of the time and takes advantage of his generosity and his money. Klipspringer uses Gatsby's piano, eats his food, and participates in his parties but seems to have no actual feelings for the man at all. When Gatsby dies Klipspringer disappears, but he does call the house once, not to pay his respects for Gatsby's death, but to tell Nick that he left a pair of his tennis shoes at the house, and he would like to get them back. Klipspringer also does not bother to attend the funeral.

Mr. and Mrs. McKee

Chester McKee and his wife are guests at the impromptu party that Tom throws in his New York love nest. Chester is a photographer whom Nick finds to be incredibly boring and self-centered. He tries to act above his class and says that he has been to a party at the home of Jay Gatsby whom he has heard many rumors about. Mrs. McKee gives the impression that she and Chester have a great marriage, when Myrtle complains about her own marriage, but Nick can tell that their relationship is just as toxic as all the others.

Catherine

Catherine is Myrtle's sister. She is another guest at the party in Tom's New York apartment. Catherine makes a big show of not being a drinker, and, for some reason, she seems very protective of the fancy furniture in Tom's love nest apartment. Despite the fact that Catherine says she does not drink, she is totally inebriated the night that Myrtle is killed. She also adamantly denies that Myrtle was having an affair behind George's back, so she has no idea what would make George go into the rage that caused him to kill Gatsby and then himself.

Mr. Gatz

Henry Gatz is the father of Jay Gatsby. When Nick informs him of his son's death he goes on and on about how wonderful Jay was and all of the goals and ambition he had as a young boy. He thought that his son had a tremendous amount of potential to really make his mark on the world. Jay had told Nick that his whole family was dead, but Nick finds out that Jay actually purchased Henry's home for him. Despite the fact that Jay rarely spoke to, or of, his father Henry came to Long Island to attend the funeral. This is ironic as the person who Jay spent his time loving and doting on, Daisy, did not bother to attend the funeral, or even acknowledge his death.

Dan Cody

Dan Cody was Jay's best friend and mentor. He was a millionaire and traveled on a yacht. Jay rowed himself out to the yacht one day to tell Dan that the wind was coming in, and Dan took Jay aboard as his first mate, assistant, sometimes babysitter, and basic Jack of all trades. Dan was a drunk, which is one of the reasons that Jay does not drink often. When he died, his will stated that Jay was to inherit everything from him, but his mistress, Ella Kaye, took everything for herself and left nothing for Jay at all. Jay has a picture of Dan hanging in his West Egg mansion.

Michaelis

Michaelis is a Greek man who owns a Greek restaurant next to George Wilson's garage. He is one of the people around when Myrtle is killed, and he is there to comfort George. He also tells Nick about the accident in which the yellow car ran Myrtle over when she came running at it. Michaelis stayed with George, worried that he would do something rash. When he left in the middle of the night to take a nap George snuck out and went to Gatsby's home to kill him.

Chapter Summaries

Chapter One

The narrator has obviously grown up with privilege, as one of the first sentiments in the novel is a memory of the advice that he got once from his father; "Whenever you feel like criticizing anyone, just remember that all the people in this world haven't had the advantages that you've had." The narrator is a non-judgmental guy which makes people trust him very easily and causes them to reveal their deepest and darkest secrets to him. The narrator is a Carraway, which means that he comes from wealth, and his family is of a very high-class stock. The narrator is well-educated, as he received his Ivy League education at Yale.

Carraway (whom we soon find out is named Nick) reveals that the setting of the novel is New York City as well as East Egg and West Egg Long Island. East Egg is a very wealthy and classy area of Long Island and West Egg, while not too shabby in its own right, is where people of "new money" tend to live; this is where the narrator resides. The people who live in West Egg do not have the connections that those with "family money" have that will allow them a place in East Egg. Nick is an exception of this as his Yale education and family ties in East Egg would likely earn him a place there. It is the spring of 1922 and Nick has moved to New York to work in bonds. Nick's home is next door to a gigantic mansion which is inhabited by Mr. Gatsby, a man who is a bit of a mystery but very popular. Nick's second-cousin Daisy and her husband Tom Buchanan live in East

Egg where Nick visits them for dinner one evening. Tom is a large and aggressive man who has a ton of money, used to play football, and went to college with Nick.

Daisy and her friend Jordan Baker are lounging on the couch, dressed totally in white. As the group enjoys some cocktails Nick casually mentions his neighbor, Mr. Gatsby and Daisy seems very interested. Daisy appears to always be happy and excited about life in general, and Nick notes that she has a bruise that Tom gave her "accidentally". Tom is trying to get everyone interested in a book that he read called "The Rise of the Colored Empires" by Goddard, which supports white-supremacist views, which Tom seems to believe in. The gathering is interrupted when Tom gets a phone, and Daisy goes ballistic. As Tom and Daisy fight, Jordan reveals to Nick that Tom is having an affair, and the woman whom he is having an affair with calls the house often. Jordan tells Nick that the affair is no secret; everyone knows. Daisy comes back into the room and starts talking about her daughter, and when she was born all she wished for her was to be a "beautiful fool" because she thinks that is the best thing that a girl can be. Nick learns that Jordan is a golfer, and he is overcome by the feeling that he has heard about her before, but he cannot think of where or when; Daisy likes to joke about Nick and Jordan getting together.

When Nick returns to West Egg that evening he sees Mr. Gatsby standing on his lawn just staring into space, apparently contemplating something about his "blue lawn". Gatsby is not just staring at his lawn, however; he is looking across the bay at a green light and stretches his arms out to it.

Chapter Two

Between the Eggs and New York is a place called the "valley of ashes", which is watched over by a billboard adorned with the blue eyes of Dr. T.J. Eckleburg, an eye doctor, wearing yellow glasses. Nick and Tom are traveling to the city together, and Tom insists on stopping to see his mistress, and introducing her to Nick. His mistress is named Myrtle Wilson and her husband, George B. Wilson is an auto mechanic who owns a repair shop. They stop by the shop with the pretense of having Tom's car worked on; Tom is a total jerk to George Wilson and shoots Myrtle a not-so-cryptic message to meet with him later. George is clueless about the affair; he just thinks that Myrtle visits her sister when she goes to the city. Myrtle joins them on a train ride to the city, and, during the trip, she expresses her desire to have a puppy. Tom gladly buys Myrtle a puppy and it becomes clear that, to Myrtle, Tom's purpose is to buy her whatever she wants. Nick is extremely uncomfortable being involved on their situation and tries to leave them, but they will not allow it.

In the city, the trio heads to the apartment where Tom and Myrtle spend most of their adulterous time at Morningside Heights. They are joined at the apartment by Myrtle's sister Catherine, a man named Mr. McKee, and some others. They group lets loose a bit by playing a drinking game with cards and Tom's whiskey; this is only the second time Nick has ever been drunk in his entire life. Nick shares with everyone that he lives in West Egg, which prompts one of the inebriated people to mention Gatsby, and the amazing parties that he throws. Catherine says that she has heard Jay Gatsby is related to Kaiser Wilhelm, ruler of Germany during World War I. Catherine begins speaking quietly to Nick and tells him that Tom and Myrtle both hate their spouses, though Tom will never divorce Daisy. He seems to be telling a series of lies to Myrtle to convince her that he will eventually leave Daisy, and she should stick around, which she does. The discussion turns to the fact that people should not marry beneath their own social class, and it seems obvious that Myrtle had done just that. Nick is completely disgusted by the people surrounding him, and he wants to leave the party, but he is somewhat fascinated by the lurid scene in front of him. Myrtle keeps mentioning Daisy and Tom tells her to stop saying Daisy's name. When Myrtle cheekily responds "Daisy, Daisy, Daisy" Tom backhands her, which results in Myrtle having a broken nose. Nick is very drunk at this point and has trouble remembering how the night ends though he does recall taking a train back to Long Island at 4:00 AM.

Chapter Three

Jay Gatsby throws very elaborate parties throughout the summer, neatly every night. Most of the people who come to the parties do not know Mr. Gatsby, nor do they ever meet him, and were not invited. Nick, however, does receive an invitation to the first party he attends at Gatsby's house, via Gatsby's chauffeur. At the party, Nick sees Jordan and hears many people gossiping about Gatsby and the fact that he is rarely ever seen at his own parties. There are rumors that he may be a member of the CIA or perhaps a murderer. Nick leaves the bustle of the party, as he is not really a party kind of guy, and heads to the library. In the library, he sees an owl-eyed man looking at the books in awe of how many there are; he tells Nick that he came into the library because he has not been sober in a week and he thought that a library would sober him up as good as anything.

When Nick leaves the library he meets a man who thinks that Nick looks familiar. As they are chatting, they find that both served in World War I and Nick learns that the man he is speaking to is none other than Jay Gatsby himself. Nick is surprised to find that Gatsby is about the same age as he is; he had assumed that Gatsby would be an older man. Gatsby excuses himself from his conversation with Nick to take a telephone call and tell his butler to get Jordan because he wants to have a private conversation with her. Nick observes the people at the party and sees a woman with red hair playing the piano and crying to the point that her black mascara is running down her cheeks. He also sees that all of the couples at the party are fighting, as the men are not allowed to look at all of the hot young women and the wives are upset that the men want to look at all of the hot young women.

When Jordan comes back from her talk with Gatsby, she talks about the "tantalizing" news she has just heard, but she does not elaborate and instead excuses herself for the night and asks Nick to come visit her at her aunt's home. Gatsby bids goodnight and confirms that he and Nick have plans the next day to go up in his "hydroplane". As Nick is leaving he sees a car leaving the driveway has run into the wall, and lost a wheel; the driver appears to be the owl-eyed man from the library. It turns out that he was not the driver; instead it was the other person in the car with him, but it is not immediately obvious who that is.

Nick continues on with his daily routine for the first half of summer and does not see Jordan again until summer is about half over. They begin hanging out together quite often, but Nick does not feel that he is in love with her. Jordan tells Nick a small lie one day and he remembers the thing that had come to mind about her the night they met; he had heard once that she cheated in a golf tournament. Nick decides that women cannot be blamed for their dishonesty. Nick also notices that Jordan is not a good driver and when he asks her to be careful she says she doesn't need to be careful, as long as everyone else is. She also tells Nick that she does not like careless people and that is why she likes him so much. From that moment, Nick is hooked on Jordan and knows that it is time for his to break off whatever he has with a girl back in Chicago. Nick decides that he does not know many honest people, but he is one of them.

Chapter Four

There are many guesses as to what Jay Gatsby may do for a living; the most common ones are murderer and bootlegger. Nick tells about all of the people who come to Gatsby's infamous parties, what they do for a living, and who they do it with. Gatsby comes to pick Nick up for a lunch date in a very fancy and very yellow, Rolls Royce. He tells Nick a little about himself; his parents were from the Midwest, very wealthy, and sent him to Oxford. Nick remembers that he heard from some people, especially Jordan that there are doubts as to Gatsby's claim that he was educated at Oxford. Jay tells Nick that he grew up in San Francisco, which is apparently Midwest in his mind, and he goes on to talk about his participation in World War I. He even shows Nick a medal that he received in the war that says "Major Jay Gatsby" on it as well as a photo of himself and some other guys at Oxford. Nick decides that he believes Gatsby, despite the doubts of the general public.

Gatsby, after being unfailingly kind to Nick, asks him for a favor. Nick feels as though he has been played for a fool by Gatsby just to get something in return, but he listens anyway. Gatsby wants Nick to speak to Jordan for him, but he does not tell him what about. Jay is further annoyed, by the way, he is being treated by Gatsby. When Gatsby is pulled over by a policeman he simply tells the man who he is and he is let off the hook; just like that. When the two men get to the city, Nick is introduced to Mr. Wolfsheim, Gatsby's business partner. Nick feels that there is something slightly off about this business pairing, as

Wolfsheim is a shady character; he supposedly fixed the World Series of 1919 and he also wears cufflinks which are made from human molars. Nick sees Tom Buchanan across the room and heads over to introduce Gatsby to him, but Gatsby has disappeared.

Later that day Nick meets up with Jordan who spills the beans about the history between Gatsby and Daisy. In October 1917, Daisy met Gatsby who was a young officer, while she was basically at the top tier of high society and eighteen-years-old. When Gatsby had to leave Daisy's family forbade her from going to say goodbye to him which caused Daisy to confine herself to her bedroom in anger toward her parents. Daisy was upset about this until the next fall when she began to rule the social scene once again where she met Tom Buchanan. Daisy married Tom in June 1919, probably because he was extremely wealthy, though she almost called the wedding off. On the eve of her wedding day, she was drunk and waved a letter in the air telling Jordan that she had changed her mind about the marriage. The message was never delivered, and Daisy and Tom were married; in April 1920, they welcomed a baby girl. After the honeymoon Daisy seemed to be head over heels for Tom, but as rumor has it Tom began cheating on her immediately with a hotel maid, amongst others. Daisy heard about Gatsby again about six weeks ago and started asking questions about him immediately; she decided that he was the same Jay Gatsby that she had fallen in love with when she was eighteen. Jordan tells Nick that Gatsby bought his house so that he could be close to Daisy, and he has a plan for Nick to invite Daisy over one day, without Tom, and Jay will just casually stop by and be reunited with her.

Chapter Five

Nick returns home after he has spoken to Jordan and he finds that Gatsby is there waiting for him. Gatsby seems very excited though he tries to act like he is not and play it cool. Gatsby tells Nick that he has an opportunity for him to make some extra money if he would like, but Nick declines and pretends that he is far too busy to take on any more responsibilities at the moment. When the day comes for Gatsby to be reunited with Daisy he is very nervous and obsesses over the smallest details, as though nothing can be perfect enough for her. Daisy gets there and again Nick comments on how unique her voice is and how it always sounds super excited. Nick tried to leave Gatsby and Daisy alone together, but he can hear the awkward silence and decides to rejoin them. Gatsby pulls Nick aside and starts flipping out about how everything is going terribly, and it is not working out nearly the way he had hoped. Nick tells him that Daisy probably just feels uncomfortable, and perhaps she would feel slightly more comfortable if she couldn't clearly hear them talking about her from the next room.

When Gatsby goes back in to see Daisy, Nick leaves the room and goes outside to stand in the rain while they get reacquainted. He comes back in, and Gatsby looks very happy and satisfied while Daisy is in tears; supposedly all they did was talk. Nick and Jay look at Gatsby's house in awe of all of it and decide to explore to look at all of the nice things. Gatsby lets it slip that he had to save up for three years to buy the house and everything inside of it, despite telling Nick earlier that he inherited his money; Gatsby is defensive and uncomfortable when Nick mentions this fact. Nick realizes that the only reason that Gatsby purchased such an extravagant house is because he was trying to impress Daisy. Nick realizes that the green light Gatsby was looking out at must have represented Daisy to him and now that Daisy is there the light is insignificant. As they are going through the house, they come across a picture which Gatsby says is of Dan Cody, who is an old friend of his. When they get back downstairs a man named Klipspringer plays "The Love Nest" on the piano and Nick leaves the newly reacquainted couple alone.

Chapter Six

A guy who writes for a newspaper in the city comes to see Gatsby to try to get him to speak about himself, as there are many rumors going around. Nick tells the reader the truth about Gatsby, which he does not actually find out until much later but wants to talk about now. Gatsby was born James Gatz to a very poor family. At the age of seventeen, he changes his name to Jay Gatsby and rows himself out to a yacht owned by Dan Cody (the man in the picture) to let him know that the wind is coming in. Dan takes Jay aboard as his steward, skipper, sometimes babysitter, and basic Jack of all trades. Dan is basically Jay's best friend for a long time. Cody had written in his will that Jay was to inherit all of his money; unfortunately, Cody's mistress decides to keep everything for herself and Jay gets nothing.

Nick is at Jay's home when three people stop by; a man named Sloane, a girl, and Tom Buchanan. Gatsby makes it a point to entertain these people although they stopped by unannounced and unexpectedly. Gatsby knows that Tom is Daisy's wife, and now that Gatsby thinks that he has secured Daisy once again he taunts Tom a bit, saying to him "I know your wife". Tom instantly dislikes Gatsby and Gatsby goes on toying with him. He asks the trio if they would stay for dinner and while the men refuse and seem wholly uninterested the woman asks if Gatsby would like to join them for dinner instead. Gatsby agrees, much to the dismay of the men, but when he returns downstairs after getting ready they have already left; Nick thinks this much be humiliating for Gatsby.

The next weekend Daisy and Tom come to a party at
Gatsby's home together. Gatsby keeps introducing
Tom to people as "the polo player" just to get on his
nerves. Daisy and Gatsby sneak off to Nick's house to
have some alone time together. When dinner rolls
around, Tom moves himself to another table, and
Daisy knows that he is going over there to flirt with a
girl who she describes as "common but pretty". Daisy
even gives Tom her gold pencil just in case he has to
write something down, knowing that he is likely
getting her phone number or giving her the address to
his love nest in the city. Nick feels as though this
party is much different from the past parties he has
been to at Gatsby's as everyone seems to be quite
hostile and very drunk.

There is a famous actress at the party who everyone
seems to have a bit of a fascination with, especially
the director she is there with who leans in to kiss her
neck. Daisy thinks that West Egg is a crude place and
is not at all impressed with the sort of people who are
at the party, except the actress of course; though she
pretends to be greatly interested in and impressed by
everything as soon as Tom begins to knock it. Tom's
desire is to know the absolute truth about Gatsby,
which entails how Gatsby came about his money
because money is all that matters to Tom. Daisy
seems insistent and certain that Gatsby's money
comes from drugs; she and Tom leave the party
together. Nick is at the party until the very end, and
he speaks to Gatsby who is frustrated with Daisy; all

he wants is for Daisy to tell Tom that she never loved him. Nick tells Gatsby that the past cannot be repeated by Gatsby does not buy it. He recalls being eighteen and wanting to take in everything that surrounds Daisy including herself, her culture, and her wealth. Nick is suddenly reminded of something he has not thought about in a long time, but he cannot remember exactly what it is.

Chapter Seven

When the next Saturday comes Gatsby stays locked up in his room and does not throw a party. He has fired every one of his servants and hired new ones whom he hopes will not spread gossip about him. Daisy comes by to have an affair with Gatsby most afternoons, much to Gatsby's delight. He sends Nick to East Egg to hang out at the Buchanan house where he finds Daisy and Jordan hanging out on the couch in their white dresses and listening to Tom talk to his mistress on the phone. When Gatsby shows up Daisy asks Tom to go into the other room to make some drinks and when he does she begins to kiss Gatsby passionately and tells him that she loves him. Daisy's daughter comes into the room for a moment before she is ushered out by the nanny and Gatsby tries to hide his disappointment that Daisy and Tom have a child.

The group has cocktails together, and the atmosphere is very strained. It is extremely hot out, but Daisy says to Gatsby "You always look so cool", which Nick explains to the reader means "I love you" in Daisy speak. Unfortunately, Tom knows Daisy speak so the atmosphere becomes even more strained after her comment. They decide to grab some whiskey and go into town, hoping that it will relieve the tension though it certainly will not. As everyone is getting ready to go Gatsby and Nick begin to talk about Daisy's voice again, and agree that it is "full of money". Daisy and Gatsby ride together in the Buchanan's blue car while Tom drives Gatsby's yellow car, accompanied by Nick and Jordan. Tom comes to the realization that his wife is having an affair with Jay and also that Nick and Jordan are aware of the affair. They stop to get gas at Wilson's station where Wilson reveals that he needs money to move out West because he has learned that his wife is having an affair, though he does not know it is with Tom. Nick sees the bespectacled eyes looking down at them from the billboard and notices that another set of eyes are watching as well; the eyes of Myrtle Wilson looking down from a window. Myrtle is staring at Jordan, obviously thinking that Jordan must be Tom's wife, and Tom realizes that he does not have control over either of his two women anymore.

The group ends up at the Plaza Hotel in a suite where tensions are higher than ever. Tom comes right out and accuses Gatsby of never attending Oxford; Gatsby admits that he did attend Oxford but only for a short time. Tom explodes and reveals to everyone that he knows about the affair; he seems absolutely appalled at the idea that his wife would have an affair with a "nobody", more so than the fact that she is having an affair. Gatsby realizes that Daisy is not going to tell Tom she never loved him, so he announces it instead. Tom refutes this and admits that he loves her as well, despite his numerous affairs. Daisy tells Tom that he is a disgusting person and finally admits that she never loved him. Tom reminds her of the times he did nice things for her, like carry her over a puddle, so she doesn't ruin her shoes, and she admits that she did love him once but does not anymore. Gatsby freaks out and tells Tom that Daisy is leaving him and Tom retaliates by telling everyone that Gatsby is a bootlegger, which he denies and gets defensive about.

Daisy decides it is time to leave and she and Gatsby ride together in Gatsby's yellow car. Through all of this excitement, Nick remembers that it is his 30th birthday. Tom, Nick, and Jordan take the Buchanan's blue car and make a pit stop at Wilson's on their way home. When they get there, it is obvious that something terrible has just happened. Michaelis, neighbor to the Wilsons, tells the group that Myrtle ran outside in a fury when she saw a yellow car and the car ran her over, killing her. It is apparent to the group that the car in question belongs to Gatsby and when the policeman interviews Tom he is sure to remind them that his own car is blue, not yellow. On the drive back home, Tom says that Gatsby is a coward for hitting Myrtle and then driving off. Back at the Buchanan house Gatsby waits for Tom to get home because he wants to make sure that he does not erupt in violence toward Daisy. Gatsby tells Nick that Daisy was driving, but he is prepared to tell everyone that he was the one driving and take the blame for the whole thing. Nick sees Tom and Daisy have an intimate moment together and realizes that they have gotten back together. He sees Gatsby watching over the house still, but Nick observes that he is really "watching over nothing".

Chapter Eight

Gatsby waits outside the Buchanan house all night long, but nothing exciting happens, as Nick knew it wouldn't. In the morning, Nick tells Gatsby that it would probably be wise for him to disappear for a while in light of recent events. Gatsby tells Nick that he could not possibly leave Daisy now and then he tells Nick his life story, which Nick already revealed to the reader in chapter six. In addition to previously revealed details, Nick finds out that Gatsby had never met a "good girl" like Daisy before, and he was immediately taken by her. At first he just wanted to fool around with her but then he fell in love. He felt extremely uncomfortable inside of Daisy's home and inside of her world because he was not wealthy or cultured as she was. Gatsby misled Daisy when they were younger, promising her a secure future though he really had nothing to offer her other than love. When Gatsby was in the war he earned medals, and did a good job, but he could not wait to get home; unfortunately for him, he ended up at Oxford instead of going straight home and Daisy married Tom because she was sick of waiting for Jay. Gatsby is convinced that Daisy still loves him and that the two can build a life together.

One of Gatsby's servants comes by and tells him that he is going to have the pool drained, but Gatsby does not see the point as he has not used it that summer. As Nick is leaving he tells Gatsby that the East Egg crowd is totally rotten, and Gatsby is worth more than all of them put together. This is interesting because Nick tells the reader that he never once actually approved of Gatsby. Jordan gives Nick a phone call later, but there is a negative vibe between the two of them, and it becomes apparent that they will no longer be seeing one another. Nick does not seem to want anything to do with Jordan or her crowd of people.

Nick found out from someone that Wilson found out about his wife's affair when he found a fancy dog collar in her room and also found some bruises on her face, both of which were courtesy of Tom. Wilson decided that the person who was driving the yellow car must have been the man who Myrtle was having an affair with, and he needs to find that man to get his revenge. Wilson ends up at Gatsby's home and sees that Gatsby is swimming in his pool, ironically. There are shots fired, and Nick runs over to Gatsby's home; it seems as though Wilson killed Gatsby and then committed suicide.

Chapter Nine

Nick deals with the scene at Gatsby including the police and photographers and then he tries to get in touch with Daisy. He finds out that the Buchanan's have moved away and have not left a forwarding address to reach them at. Nick makes a strong attempt to find some friends or family of Gatsby's to inform of his death and invite to his funeral, but he cannot find any. He hears a message on the answering machine at Gatsby's that confirms his involvement in illegal activities; he also hangs up on a man who calls stating that he wants back a pair of shoes which were at Gatsby's home. Nick does get ahold of Mr. Gatz, Jay's father, who seems to believe that his son was going to change the world someday. He reveals that Jay was always determined to break away from the life of poverty he had been raised in and to do something great with his life.

The day of the funeral is very rainy, and Nick finds that only one other person has shown up – the owl-eyed man. He and Nick discuss how awful it is that Gatsby had so many great parties, and invited so many people, yet none of them could be bothered to attend his funeral. Nick begins to think about waiting at train stations in the Midwest and decides that he, Jordan, Tom, Daisy, and Gatsby were not cut out for the East; they were all Westerners who needed to get out of the fake life they were living. He recalls an El Greco painting he saw once with a woman dressed all in white who is carried into the wrong house on a stretcher. He decides that he must move back home. Nick meets up with Jordan one last time before he heads back West and she tells him that she trusted him, but he was dishonest and was even more careless than she, as a driver. Nick tells her that as a thirty year old he is five years past being able to lie to himself under the pretense of being honorable. He also tells her that he is "half in love with her" and apologizes as he leaves.

A while later Nick runs into Tom Buchanan who has come back into town. He tells Nick that he was the one who told Wilson that the yellow car belonged to Jay Gatsby. Nick wonders if he should tell Tom that Daisy was the one driving the car; he always wonders if Daisy really was the one driving the car or if Gatsby had lied to him. Nick comes to the realization that Tom and Daisy were actually a lot alike; they were both extremely careless people who were not responsible enough to clean up their own messes. Nick wanders around outside Gatsby's house, on his blue lawn. He looks across the bay and sees the green light that Gatsby was always staring at; the green light on Daisy's house. He determines that Gatsby's problem was that he was always reaching out toward his dream, rather than realizing his dream was all in his past.

Made in the USA
Lexington, KY
28 November 2015